Oceans

A & C BLACK • LONDON

Oceans

contents

First published 2002 in Australia by Blake Education Pty Ltd

This edition published 2003 in the United Kingdom by
A&C Black Publishers Ltd, 37 Soho Square, London W1D 3QZ
www.acblack.com

ISBN 0-7136-6598-X

A CIP record for this book is available from the British Library.

Written by Katy Pike and Maureen O'Keefe
Science Consultant: Dr Will Edwards, James Cook University
Design and layout by The Modern Art Production Group
Photos by Photodisc, Stockbyte, John Foxx, Corbis, Imagin,
Artville Digital Vision and Corel

UK Series Consultant: Julie Garnett

Printed in Hong Kong by Wing King Tong Co Ltd

A & C Black uses paper produced with elemental chlorine-free pulp,
harvested from managed sustainable forests.

Oceans and Seas

Earth is known as the Blue Planet because water covers so much of its surface. Oceans cover more than 70 percent of the Earth.

The Pacific Ocean is the largest and deepest ocean. It covers one-third of the planet. The Atlantic Ocean is the second largest ocean, followed by the Indian Ocean.

Two smaller oceans surround the **Poles**. The Southern Ocean surrounds the South Pole. The smallest ocean, the Arctic Ocean, circles the North Pole. The Arctic Ocean is so cold that it's covered with ice for six months each year.

Southern Ocean

Smaller areas of the ocean are called seas. The Mediterranean and the Caribbean are the largest seas.

All the oceans are connected and water flows between them. You could sail around the world without ever touching land.

4

Oceans on Earth can be seen from space.

5

Oceans of the World

BERING SEA

NORTH SEA

ATLANTIC
OCEAN

CARIBBEAN SEA

PACIFIC
OCEAN

ARCTIC OCEAN

BALTIC SEA

BLACK SEA

MEDITERRANEAN
SEA

RED SEA

PACIFIC
OCEAN

INDIAN
OCEAN

CORAL SEA

TASMAN SEA

SOUTHERN OCEAN

Coasts

The coast is where the land meets the sea. Coasts can be sandy beaches, jagged cliffs or rocky shores. Coastlines are shaped by the constant forces of sea, wind and rain.

Coastlines constantly change. Waves wash rocks into the ocean. These rocks are then worn down into smaller and smaller pieces, becoming sand. This wearing down is called **erosion**.

Some rocks remain as cliffs, **headlands** and rocky ground. Headlands are cliffs that jut out into the ocean. Headlands can be made of hard rock such as granite. Even hard rock is slowly worn down by waves. Rocky ground along the coast wears away at different rates, forming rock pools.

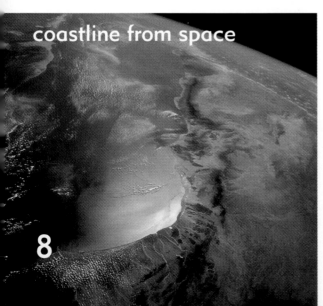

coastline from space

The movement of water and sand also changes the shoreline. Sandy beaches cover many coasts. Storms and tides move sand along the beach or out into the ocean. Large amounts of sand come to the coast from inland, washed into the sea by rivers.

The lighthouse warns boats to stay away from this rocky shore.

A sandy beach forms where soft rock has been eroded.

Hard rock creates a headland that sticks out into the ocean.

GO FACTS

FIRST!

The earliest lighthouses were fires built on hillsides to guide ships.

9

Waves, Tides and Currents

The ocean is constantly moving. Waves move across its surface. The sea level rises and falls with the tides. Water flows in currents around the Earth.

Most waves are made by the wind. A breeze creates a small ripple while strong winds create large, powerful waves. The speed and size of a wave depends on the wind's strength, how long it has been blowing, and how far it has come across the ocean. When winds blow across a large stretch of ocean, they create smooth, travelling waves called a **swell**.

The 'pull' of the moon and the sun on Earth causes the tides. This pull is called **gravity**. During a high tide, the sea moves further up onto the land. At low tide, the water moves away from the land.

Currents are like rivers in the ocean. Cold water currents travel to the Equator from the Poles. Warm water currents flow back to the Poles.

When the tide goes out, the ground around this tree dries out.

TALLEST!
The tallest wave ever measured was in July 1958, at Lituya Bay, Alaska. It was 500 metres high.

Making Waves

A wave travels through the water. After rising and falling, most of the water remains in the same place.

You can see this happen.

You will need:
- long tank or baby bath
- two toys — one that floats and one that sinks to the bottom
- water
- wooden paddle

1 Fill the tank with water.

2 Place both toys in the tank.

3 Make small waves close to the surface with the paddle.

4 Lower your paddle in the water and make larger waves.

What happens to the toys?

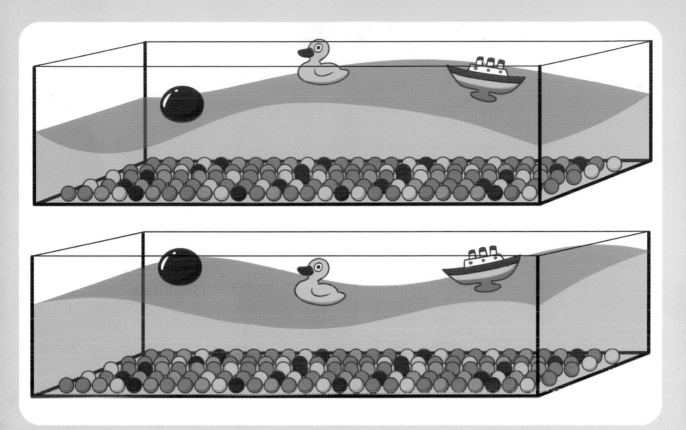

As the wave passes, the duck moves up and down but remains in the same position.

When floating on a swell, the same thing happens to people.

13

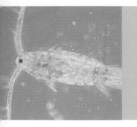

Sea Food

Plants are an essential part of the ocean's food chains. Some sea creatures eat plants. Other animals are carnivores that eat other sea creatures.

Food chains in the ocean begin with plankton. Plankton is a mixture of tiny animals and **algae**. Like all plants, the algae use the sun's energy to make food. Very small crustaceans feed on the tiny algae and, together, they are known as plankton.

Many different food chains occur in the ocean. Small creatures, such as **krill** and shrimps, eat tiny plankton. Fish, squid and octopuses feed on shrimps. These are then eaten by even larger fish, sharks and whales.

Some food chains are shorter. Swarms of krill number in the millions. The largest sea creature, the blue whale, feeds mainly on krill.

Dead creatures sink to the ocean floor, providing food for many other animals.

octopus

plankton

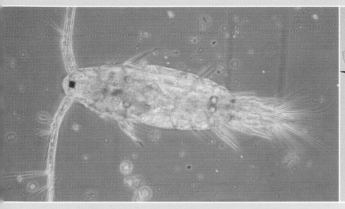

microscopic crustacean

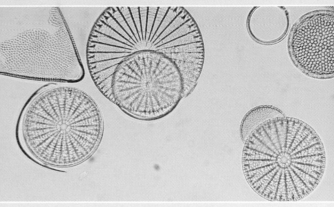

microscopic algae

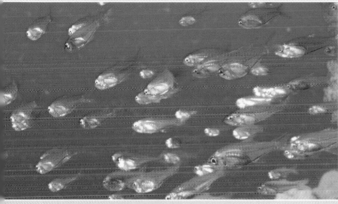

glass fish

shrimp

hammerhead shark

blue striped grunt

GO FACTS

DID YOU KNOW?
A blue whale can eat four tons of krill a day.

killer whale

15

Life in the Ocean

The ocean habitat has three layers or zones. More than 90 percent of all marine life lives in the sunlit zone.

Life at the top — The Sunlit Zone (0–200 metres)

The sunlit **zone** gets plenty of light, which is essential for the growth of plants. Algae and seaweed grow in this zone.

Most marine animals live in this upper sunlit layer of the ocean. This is where you will find large numbers of fish and other sea creatures. Seabirds and marine mammals feed on the rich food found in these waters.

Schools of fish, such as silver snappers and sardines, live here. Larger fish, such as cod and tuna, use their speed to catch and eat smaller fish. Most sharks hunt in the sunlit zone but some are deep-water hunters.

school of snapper

Sea turtles live in the sunlit zone.

Sea lions hunt for fish and squid.

Coral reefs grow in the sunlit zone.

The Deep Ocean

The ocean depths get colder and darker. This is the largest habitat in the world but, as food is scarce, fewer animals live here.

Life in the middle — The Twilight Zone (200–1 000 metres)

Only dim, blue light reaches this zone so plants can't live here. Creatures must eat other animals or catch food that falls from above. Many fish that live in this zone have big eyes that look upwards.

Deep-sea fish can go for long periods without food. Many of them, such as the viperfish, swim with their jaws wide open, ready for the next meal.

Some fish at this level produce their own light. Lanternfish use light to find their prey.

The ocean depths — The Midnight Zone (1 000–4 000 metres)

Most fish at this level are small and don't eat very often. Gulper eels have huge mouths and elastic stomachs so they can eat things as large as themselves. The anglerfish uses light to lure prey, then gulps them into its gaping jaws.

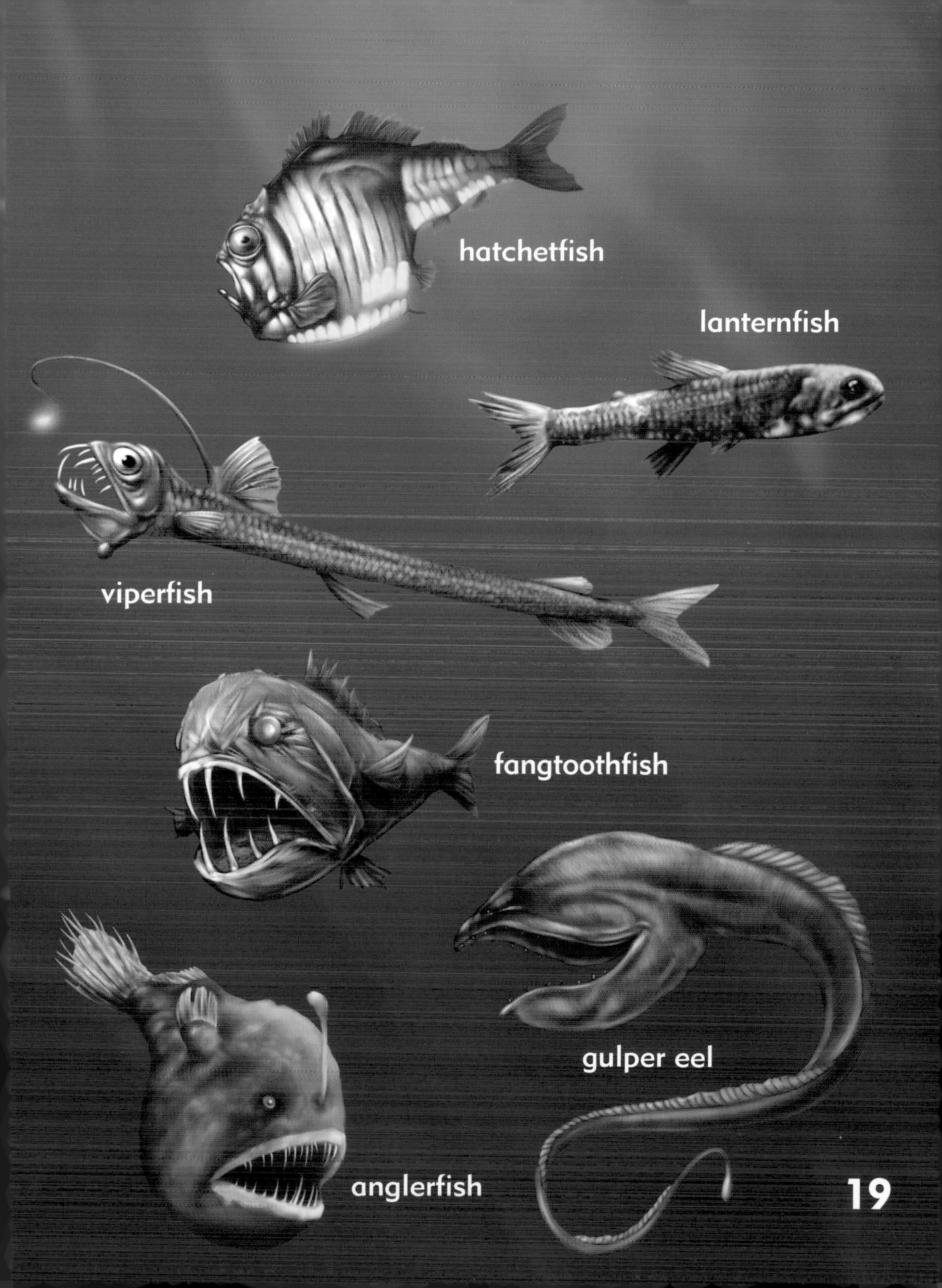

hatchetfish

lanternfish

viperfish

fangtoothfish

gulper eel

anglerfish

19

The ocean floor has many of the same features you find on land. Mountain ranges, volcanoes, deep trenches and wide, flat plains are all found on the ocean floor.

Continents and islands are surrounded by **continental shelves**. These shelves slope slowly downwards from the shore. In many places these shelves end in underwater cliffs that drop to the deep ocean.

Chains of underwater volcanoes, known as **seamounts**, exist on all ocean floors. Some islands are seamounts that have risen out of the ocean. The Hawaiian Islands are at the end of a chain of underwater volcanoes.

Hawaii seen from space

Ocean trenches are very deep cuts in the ocean floor. The Mariana Trench is the deepest place on Earth.

Bubbling, hot water pours out of deep-sea vents known as black smokers. Tube worms and giant clams live around these vents.

20

Animals that live around black smokers can withstand very high temperatures.

TALLEST!
When measured from the ocean floor, Hawaii's Mauna Kea rises more than 9 145 metres, making it the tallest mountain on Earth.

Strange creatures can live on the ocean floor.

How Deep Can We Go?

Who or what		Depth
Scuba diver with oxygen tank		50 m
The JIM suit		500 m
Deep-sea rescue vessel		1525 m
Deep-sea submersible— Alvin		4000 m
Deep-sea submersible— Trieste		10 860 m

Glossary

algae	simple, non-flowering plants that grow in water
continental shelf	the shallow, sloping ocean floor around continents and islands
current	a flow of water moving in one direction
erosion	gradual wearing away of something
food chain	a series of living things in which each one feeds on the next
gravity	the pulling force that Earth, the sun, and the moon exert
habitat	the usual place where something lives
headland	a rocky cliff that juts out to sea
krill	shrimp-like crustaceans
Poles	the furthest northern and southern points on Earth
seamount	an underwater volcanic mountain
swell	a travelling wave on the open sea
zone	a defined area

Index